THE REEF

PHOENIX POETS

A SERIES EDITED BY ALAN SHAPIRO

ELIZABETH ARNOLD

the reef

THE UNIVERSITY OF CHICAGO PRESS
Chicago and London

Elizabeth Arnold's poems and essays have appeared in *TriQuarterly*, *Sagetrieb*, *Chicago Review*, *Carolina Quarterly,* and other magazines. She was book editor and wrote the afterword for the first edition of Mina Loy's novel, *Insel*. A fellow at the Fine Arts Work Center in Provincetown for 1997–98, she now teaches in the writing program at Warren Wilson College in Swannanoa, North Carolina.

The University of Chicago Press, Chicago 60637
The University of Chicago Press, Ltd., London

08 07 06 05 04 03 02 01 00 99   1 2 3 4 5

ISBN: 0-226-02736-8 (cloth)
ISBN: 0-226-02737-6 (paper)

Arnold, Elizabeth, 1958–
The reef / Elizabeth Arnold.
p. cm.
ISBN 0-226-02736-8 (cloth : alk. paper). – ISBN 0-226-02737-6 (paper : alk. paper)
1. Body, Human–Poetry. 2. Diseases–Poetry. I. Title.
PS3551.R4846R44 1999
811'.54–dc21   98-17505
CIP

∞ The paper used in this publication meets the minimum requirements of the American National Standard for Information Sciences—Permanence of Paper for Printed Library Materials, ANSI Z39.48-1992.

For my mother and father, and for Jack

Change alone is unchanging. . . .
The life of fire comes from the death of earth. The life of air comes from the death of fire. The life of water comes from the death of air. The life of earth comes from the death of water.

—Heraclitus

. . . and so I sing, because I am afraid.

—Emily Dickinson

THE REEF

Introit

Tremendous blocks of ice-
smooth turquoise-tinted slabs
—not quite ice yet, not even
slabs but only seeming
to be, through the slightly
convex surface of the rushing
(but not breaking) roiling
water of the stream—go past
as blurred or sharp, depending
on how fast whatever guides
the eye can follow then
flip back, catching the next
unbounded segment of the stream
that's hurtling down the giant
runnel it has tunneled at
god knows how long, the finger-
numbing force not rumbling
as you might expect, but
whispering at a pitch so high
it's almost out of range—
a sound as if of exhalation,
breathing over my whole sense
the air the stream has cooled,

a stream nearing its hectic end
where it will spill
everything it has into
the waiting, open-ended
once-lake arm of ocean,
the forest-green fjord—
as earlier, uncountable
millennia ago, it broke
the barrier of dirt and rock,
crashed through or slowly rubbed
until the land dissolved
and flooded through itself
beyond beyond.

I

Whither I go, thou canst not follow me. . . .

Walking toward the ginkgo trees,
their yellow, fan-shaped leaves
around their trunks in rings,
my feet sink where the moles dug,
pushed through darkness near the top,
the earth buckling behind
as if it had been hoed from underneath.

I wonder how the dead go,
blind at first to what is near,
until the force incomparable
will turn on how they know,
displacing ten-ton beams
of their attention, thundering them
from one world to the next.

•

He opened the bird and out flew 54 post-mortem bees,
out of a crow's craw, shot and fallen seconds before
during the fatal feeding, steam still rising from the corpse
into the gap of its last flight.

Where now the bees are,
straggling as before, when eaten, having broken ranks
with home in sight. The gunshot spreading through the woods in rings,
the bees again go staggering up and this time make it.

Hunter/gatherer, farmer in this wilderness,
Crèvecoeur must have smiled as he turned back, the crow
limp on his shoulder—at the wonder of it, the new world's
seemingly endless hoard, its numbers forever self-renewing.
Counting all he saw until his numbers petered out,
he headed home, carrying what he could of the meat,
with the liquid light to come.

•

Her stallion, black-bay, beautiful, had disappeared.
Kernan and Bo and Nancy backed the jeeps out,
tore down the sand road, found him dead in the middle of a swamp.
They had to use a crane to haul him out;
one of his legs broke off.

Which made me think of another story Kernan told,
the one about the aunt with cancer—how
her doctors, trying to outrun fast proliferating cells,
cut first one arm off, then the other, then both legs:
I saw her in the bed like that.

•

What window opens from what's seen? What door
cracks onto what? Door, window, song—
what physical vibration for the eye or ear
could hack a way through fact?

Sacrificed for some such sign, the shamans'
lonely victims, disembowled and hurled through air,
would never see the words their own intestines spelled
above them as they fell.

Later, when the bowels had dried—stretched taut from the altar
down to the low cliff's foot—the priests came back
to listen to the wind whistling through
the leathery strings.

They hoped for god talk, caught where the victims' souls
had left their tortured bodies. The shaman
I heard interviewed admitted they got nothing
but their questions back,

which they would ask and ask and listen for
until they died, the echoes opening
onto nothing, dispersed among and by the dust,
the sun-singed scrub, the sky.

•

It was no time, it was in a dream
that in-time won in spite of love
and let love go. No scream broke
the long glide home.

Or so we thought it, the car gone
out of control. We sat there quiet,
waiting, my sister and I, while the car bombed
through the air

over the embankment. It took forever.
It was a place to talk. We spoke freely
and with point, though we had fought,
ten years apart.

I told her there what I had always
wished to say but had not known,
and she could hear. But when we did
not die, the car

crashing anyway and everything
we'd found to say again was lost,
her face was set, and we stood looking
at the wreck.

•

The afternoon I learned a close friend's mother,
having fought the thing for months, was close to death
from cancer, five miles away we stood upstairs,
the day's light pulling back behind the leafless trees
to the southwest of our house. Your face flat as an owl's—
you'd lost your father just a year before—
you said you thought of dying as a walk through woods,
palmetto, scrub oak, pine, the going getting harder
as the tangle of vines got thicker, brambles grabbing
at your feet, chest, face, the sky almost completely
blocked by branches. You'd keep tugging at the undergrowth,
you said, keep trudging—without spirit but persistent—on,
as if despite your doubt there were an opening
on the other side, though nothing recognizable in sight,
and then the panic—feel it in your gut—then stop
to listen, look, in the middle of this nowhere, lost.

•

Touch another's arm and the blood flows, floats
you over. Otherwise the circuit's closed.

•

Walleyed from the start, my vision lurched,
doubling the crib's bars, then swerved back.

I hid inside the columned curve of banister
and watched and listened—voices
hollow as a flute, words blurred
into music—when the world paled, came up double,

so that running hard for one of them
I had to reach my arms out like the blind,
ready to collide, or run right through.

•

How between two people
                                        there begins
a symphony of looks, of
                    little comments, smiles,
refrainings from—
                              even if the person's just a friend
(but not a relative, not like this).

It happens over days,
                              or months, or years,
                                                  a letter maybe,
the not responding right away
                                              refining the
                                        relationship
with every shifting in my chair, the turning of my head away
          and back
                              so that you see the delicacy,
                                                            fragility,
even move your hand toward—

which takes six months to measure,
                                                  six more
percolating in the soul
                                        the body's brine,
                                                            a mix
centrifugality will sort and offer back:

I tilt my head at it

to catch

the switches sifting through,

a little puff

across the surface,

pricks of light.

A couple of years later, you smile back.

•

Unlike Bacon's other portraits—George Dyer's face
stuck in a table in Paris,
or Isabel Rawthorne's primal nose holes (minus the nose),
the mouth pulled like a sloppy rubber band
across her face, each picture
starting some new ghost
or fury, as if he saw no limit to its interaction with the meat—

the 1973 self-portrait, as if the man
were all one piece, holds still,
a yellow plastic watch around the wrist, the face
like it's been smashed but nothing's broken,
its flesh pulled like some putty, up,
and dented. But then the hands,
trying to hug the knees, are blurred and even disappear in places,

moving the eye back to the face that, in another study,
was half blown away,
leaving only Bacon's own characteristic cobwebbed x-rayed look,
where everything that happens
happens into nothingness.
As in this later portrait,
where below the yellow watch the hands go out.
And then the shirt (you see it now) and what arises

from the table farther over, from the hat
or bowl—our everydayness—unstopped
by the edges of the canvas, a column of blackness

threatening, now that he's older, to fill in the whole
window Bacon's opened, for himself, for us,
of himself fearing falling through.

When you look through air
into the water, arms
and legs will magnify
or shrink, or shift,
maybe to the right
of where the arm or leg,
solid as rock and cold,
actually is.
My mother's legs looked fat,
her bathing-suit skirt
fluttering at the surface.
"Swim to me," she said,
and thinking I could make it
from the edge to where she stood,
although I had not learned yet
how to turn my head
to breathe, and the pool was deep,
I nodded to her. She
smiled back, then looked away,
turning now to someone else,
and I pushed off,
pulling my body through
the turquoise mass. Until
I saw her legs step back
and back, mechanically,
severed somehow
from her upper half,
which occupied the normal world
above the surface, filled
with all the summer smells
and chatter, other mothers,

kids my age, the sun—
all suddenly gone
as I struggled toward her
backing up, my mother.
Would she bend and
pull me out, back
into the sunlit world?

•

Here I am a third time, lying on a metal bed in sheets.
The surgeon's tools wink blankly back against the green-tiled windowless walls.
A nurse's hand like ice in mine, I watch the doctor's mouth speak words
while all his other parts—the eyes, the shoulders, hands—say he is sorry,
he the knower, healer, doer, as he tells me it's come back,
"recurred," awakened, de-remissed. But I don't freeze; just when I hear the words
I'm more alert than even in those heady times when nothing hurts:
beginning, middle, end make one clear frame, inside of which I fit.

Back home, outdoors, I sit and stare, hearing in the usual background noise
the whistling of the front-door keyhole tighten to a buzzing moan,
which wakes me up, but this time to a storm, offshore somewhere,
a just-named hurricane spinning at the water underneath,
hurling the sky out from itself in spirals, hundreds of miles beyond
the place it started (which has, with Earth, gone past that point), folding
at higher and higher speeds the raw material, air, into its mass
until great gusts of wind enrage the oaks, send dead leaves scattering,
scuttling up the street, while cloud-bands give and take away light,
turning the world into a carnival no one escapes.

•

Rubbed till she was numb, she was consumed.
Not to say she didn't try to run away.
But like a breaking wave it widened, foamed,
passed through and over, no escape, as if she were
a wave and spreading, fanning wider, thinner,
across a beach of space, as if she were the beach,
dissolving sand in water as it took her,
who she was, this feeling—this sensation, rather:
animal. She liked it though it scared her,
who she was she was no longer, was erased.

•

You give to them your life to keep, the green-robed ones
who, padding down the hall

in green-swathed feet, come wrap you like a mummy up,
the cool hands nudging

at your wrist, your waist. They roll you, their papoose,
down glittering,

arctic tunnel-halls, then, once you're lost in sleep,
they touch your heart,

beating at its rib cage rubbery, tough young wings, then lift
your spleen free,

cradle it above the bloody cavity
and take it.

When at last they pull you from the rasping, sucking, snipping
so gently

that you love them for it, helpless newborn, wordless, wet,
you push your flesh-

thinned blind-eyed face up at them through the swimming air,
the skin-cooled beings, gods.

•

The rails' sound hurt, rasping metal wheels on tracks
against my spine it seemed, the train thundering northbound
through the dark. Sleeping on the shuddering floor,
I dreamed again of the night with all those travelers in Rome,
Chianti cherry-colored drunk, confessing (loudly)
to a stranger in a cheap hotel.

Then the light came, Orkney, bright in the cloud's glare,
the treeless whale's-head bluffs against the sea, with the wind
roaring, whistling . . .

They told me later I had died, stopped breathing.
You'd think that I'd remember, that whatever's next
would startle even out of anesthesia. But dying
can be quick, I guess, as just before they start to cut
the drug steals voices and the lights before the needle's out.

•

The black-clad, histrionic priest I never liked
leaned over me and craftily, quickly smudged my forehead
with some stuff that made me think of high school, at the beach
—*tanning butter,* that was what it felt like—and it stank
of cheap perfume. My family, in a circle around my bed,
held hands (which wasn't like them) and began to pray,
following the minister's confident, repressive lead.
A standard prayer. The words were dead. I felt possessed.
But not of what they hoped.

Another day
the over-animated aunt, the not-quite-right one, came,
bringing along a two-bit rendering of Christ—
it looked like something she'd picked up at a garage sale,
bearded, sad-eyed, pitiful for my plight—to make me
turn my hate to love.

•

The joy of accidents, of deaths, the eyebrows raised:
it's where we're rushing to, we like to hurry it along.

The news that someone known to you
has caught a fatal illness, cancer, AIDS.
The close proximity can conjure Bhopal,
Bosnia, Chernobyl—yet it's safe.

As when my best friend heard, and suddenly
her pointless teenage life took hold, took off.

For me there were the practical concerns:
thirst, for example—where's the goddammed nurse?
Insomnia. So every day this week,
and the next, and the next, I go to *that* department
for radiation, down this hall, not that one.

While beyond my hearing, friends were thrilling to
"six months to live"—only a couple of houses down,
that happening, *that*. The whispering, wondering,
camouflaged by care: what everybody wants
they "can't believe" or find "amazing"—intimacy
with death, with that which awes, appalls.

•

Waking just past dawn, I'd go (no breakfast) to the doctor's. Sitting (cold) in the waiting room in shorts, I'd hear my name. I knew the voice—nasal yet low-registered, as if it didn't have a heart. I'd stand up, slowly, follow yet hang back, knowing this time what was coming, wanting to suspend my sense of feeling well, even if it gave the bad cells time to crowd out what was left of the "good" ones. Sad defense against that marching forward of the "regimen" of chemotherapy drugs.

I could have turned around, I could have run, I could have caught the bus I heard outside.

Instead, of course, I followed the nurse into the room's box, climbed onto the metal table, lay down, looked cheerful even, opening all I was to the nurse's bruskness—her defense—for mercy, let her pat my hand for veins.

And then it came, the fluid clear as water, cold inside my hand, my arm. I felt it traveling up. And then the taste—how could it rise so fast? That taste. And as the room began to reel, I suffered her to empty the syringe, the infiltration finished in an instant, flushing through the tiniest capillaries of the skin and deep in organs, lungs, the cauliflower branches of my brain, the drugs riding the wave of blood which, racing through me as it always has, was innocently carrying forth and meaning well.

•

All day, no matter how much light poked through
the blinds in bars, I "slept," trying to outsmart nausea.
But though I gave it nothing to cough up
and kept my eyes closed tight, the body gagged,
forced out the tainted, yellow jelly cells.

•

Leaning over me, she took my head into her hands,
the short hair thick still, full beneath her fingers.

She told me she had read that pressure (from
a rubber band about the head) combined with

lowered temperatures (from ice) would sometimes
keep the drugs from killing hair roots in the scalp.

I suffered numbness, ache from cold, for her,
for hope. She only had to try it once.

•

A man who lived near Nagasaki, an old man, dying,
went to town by chance the day the bomb's flash shook the air
into a thousand thousand thousand thousand sub-
atomic missiles that shot past the daylight through him, through
the others, vaporized many, sickened thousands to their deaths,
and he was cured.

Radiation, poisons kill
the faster-growing cells (the hair roots, for example—
weeds in grass) and start them losing their integrity;
undifferentiated nuclei (like those that make up scars,
that heal), the displaced orphans angry, out for blood, for bone,
the marrow—mine near the point of insurrection. Any more drugs
they tell me, and I'll get leukemia. "We're frightened,"
the oncologists, "frightened for you—really, of you,
of your youth, because your health can turn against you
with such vigor, grow the most robust,
the quickest tumors we can't fight against and win."

•

Scars still red, a couple of stitch marks
          tight still, puckered.
No one touched me then or looked,
          or if they did,
they did it quickly, with reluctance,
          so that, ready
for reception of the colder kind,
          I'd go first,
withdraw. And later, in the house alone,
          the doorbell ringing
while I crouched behind the bed,
          and then the phone—
they'd hang up finally, redial
          immediately,
so that the ringing would start up
          again, start up
three times at least. And still that other,
          soundless bell
descends with nothing in it but
          the soul-less world
that's filled and filling up with fear.
          Which starts the
emptying out, the echoing,
          reechoing,
the nothing in this world for me.

•

Shallow-rooted moss-hung water oak, its hollow
limbless trunk, the deep-combed furrows rivering down,
appearing strong it saved me from disintegration once—
the sight of it, its sparkling leaves, the certainty
that it stood just beyond the pane.

•

II

Walk while ye have the light, lest darkness come upon you. . . .

When they (my family, family friends), frustrated, tired, cannot follow
anymore where I would take them, it's like a movie going by

I've passed beyond them   finally   I'm past their reach
I have to give them up   I've done it   without meaning to
a weight lifts   even if   for just a second

Then it's back, I'm back, they—everybody, everything,
up in it all again. Now I'm the one who's angry, tired.

•

Five years post-chemo, a knife stabbed through
my thigh. I fell in the street. No cars came
and I limped away, the pain subsiding.

It came again, of course, and again,
it woke me up at night, held me
in a ball all day. So I had the tests,

CAT scan, bone scan, MRI—
and nothing. Every test but surgery.
And the pain stayed, vivid, too exact,

inside my leg. They called me crazy
in my disbelief, then chronic,
then they sent the nurse's aid:

Chronic Pain at Twenty-Five.
So with the war vets who'd been fried,
I sank down c/o Flexeril.

The air got thick. I walked lead-footed
through it, down South 58th Street west,
the well-dressed and impoverished chic

flew both ways by me, hurrying toward
some heady goal or conquest, past
the neo-Gothic buildings,

the Lab School playground cordoned off,
then Rockefeller Chapel,
Robie House, then, to my left

the Oriental Institute where,
walking slowly by, I saw
as if I saw the Assyrian bas-relief

I always went to first, the small
but muscled man in it who stands
so stiffly, staring straight ahead.

He wears a heavy-looking rope-like braid
but doesn't seem to mind the weight.
Beside him is his horse, whose tiny

tendoned pasterns tremble, having sprung,
it seems, at just that instant
from the artist's hand, the horse's power

fully contained though on the verge of bursting out.
It was always cool in summer there,
secret as a cave. I felt,

I smelled the building's breath
as I limped past, along its heavy
high stone front, the patterned iron gates

above the marble lintel shut.

•

This time, the secretary led us through a different door, into the surgeon's office, dark compared to where they usually put me. My mother sat, I sat, sank into the antique cushioned chairs. It was cold. We waited.

Cross your legs. It moves. The leg on top. With every heart beat. That can't be normal. Or maybe it's my watching it, the noticing that's wrong. (Too afraid to ask. My mother made me come.)

She opened a magazine, closed it on her lap when the doorknob clicked. The hand and arm emerging at the widening crack I knew, the motion, short. Everything warm and cold at once, his hand rough from surgical soap. He sat behind the desk. My mother told him why we'd come. Then, shifting sharp, he made the military switch from her to me, the other grown-up in the room.

I dreaded disappointing him or anyone—I'd never tell him I was sure, if I was sure of anything, how all of what was outside threatened. Inside too. *That beating, must be mad, my body jerking to it.* I couldn't tell a man like that. My terrible weakness, mine, a full-grown girl *("You're a full-grown girl!")*, legally of age, wishing she could hide behind her mother's skirts? Afraid to answer the phone? I couldn't even say it to myself. I couldn't even know it, get anywhere near it. Only open the cabinet in the tiny upstairs bathroom, sit on the floor and stare for hours, leaning my back against the door, sawing at my wrists. But no more than a scratch! Laughable! *(You fool!)*

So when the doctor told me that the only people needing psychological help don't think they do, to please him (and myself) I nodded in relief and promised to be better from then on, be brave, be well, and swallow down the pills prescribed, the little robin's eggs.

•

A film shot backward catches fire
and is eaten into white,
the tiny crooked line part-way across
adjusting, jerking frame to frame.

•

North of New Orleans, the flat bridge low over swamp,
its seemingly endless, predictable repeat

of same-sized concrete slabs that clicked
each time I crossed a crack. I drove it in the dark,

hurtling through in a light-weight rented car,
the plastic steering wheel and knobs and switches cheap.

I passed a truck. Five minutes. Then another, going south,
a car. Exhausted from a conference in the city,

dreading the brittle cheerfulness of my hosts,
my thoughts flew past them, on to other worries

when I saw it, right in front of me
(and I was going fast): two cars crashed, no one there,

no one alive, I feared, no sirens even. So the wreck
had just occurred. I swerved around it to the left.

And then the twirling lights ahead, I saw them coming,
flying down my lane, the two-lane northbound side

of the miles and miles of bridge—the only way to get there.
So for the second time that night I missed disaster,

swerving back as the bridge became a road again,
the ground held firm beneath instead of air.

•

So what is it, then, this being human,
except just being, here on the porch,
in the last square of sunlight,
dulled from some—
as it will seem much sooner than you think—
bearable blow.
You still can feel this last heat,
the softened and flowery breeze.
You can still hear the bird's static:
lovers pairing up all over town.

•

I saved the negatives she wrote in magic marker on,
the nurse who didn't know what it was for, the sonogram:
"arms around his knees" and "baby sucking thumb," the flitching
shrimp-like fetus stopped, its back arched, gristle grinding, flexing,
pushing off.

I watched it on the tube in black and white.
My belly skin felt tight. Pretending I was pleased, I turned
my head away to cry.

•

Even when you ask it of yourself—
what happened

in a dream or in your childhood, how it felt
—the thought recedes,

the fleetest recognition triggering flight. As if
the mother follows

wiping up the mess, and when you spin around
to see,

no trace of either's there.

•

III

The wind bloweth where it listeth, and thou hearest the sound thereof, but canst not tell whence it cometh, or whither it goeth. . . .

I dreamed our birds, amazed but not confused, flew through
the opening that had always been, to them, the glass
of two french doors. They'd learned that outside was as far
as their original Peru, but still were drawn
to all the goings-on out there—wind-blown bees and leaves,
loud cawing blue jays, mockingbirds, the buzzing and the whir.
They'd perch on the inside "sills" and watch and lean,
drawing their feathers in, then fly back
to a safer perch.

But this time we forgot
and they flew out as if there'd never been an obstacle.
I watched them as they dipped and lilted up, landing
on a camphor branch, their green and cobalt blue
barely visible that high up. Then turning into specks
they left the branch and darted, disappeared.

I woke up
to the real birds' chirping, the cock bird mimicking the blue jay's taunting,
drumming his wings in flight from one side to the other of his cage.

•

It happened at a friend's house first, the lights switched off, our talking
stopped. I couldn't sleep. The blinds let bars of light in
from the street. My eyes filled up with gray, blurred black-and-white,
which blended with whatever I am made of, so that I grew,
started to be made of stone, my features sanded down,
the bony parts (hips, elbows, wrists) becoming grainy, bloated
but solid—lacking deftness, though, no art—just getting bigger,
filling up the room regardless, breaking the building's boundary
with the street, the orange-pink city sky, Lake Michigan . . .
But that distended sense, unwieldiness, a suffocating
filling-up of space, as in a crowd that's squeezed
into a narrow place, propelled by its own motor through,
the tangle of fallen bodies underfoot.

•

Because the dark meat
won't clean-up,

blood at the joints, fat
bubbling up through dirt,

a crater dug
then filled again in haste

so that a foot sticks out, a hand,
the loam

in body hair hangs
shadowing flesh.

We get it on the air waves straight:
"The knife went in my knee.

My friend, my neighbor,
childhood playmate,

in the very building
where we started school—

he stabbed me in the knee."
The translator's voice,

without affect,
as if it had

no physicality,
reflecting objectivity—

we get it straight, we say,
amazed and

satisfied,
then bow our heads and

pray sweet god
and lock our doors.

•

Could it have been the body's fault?
—its need to grow betraying me
as when my uterus contracted
faster and with increasing force
at what could not be driven out?

—or the allergy to Compazine
that made my jaw go sideways hard
until it almost broke? —when the doctor
(on-call, coming just in time)
shot Valium in my open vein?

Sixty miles per hour, blood.
Where might that river take me now, that flood?

•

A group of Baptists stood knee-deep in the St. Johns River,
their thin white robes ballooning in the wind.
They bent the big man back and pushed him under
the oak-stained water, holding him down for a few long
seemingly endless seconds so that when they let him go,
he popped up like a buoy.

As if he'd died and come again to life,
out of the murk and tangle of the holy robes.
I saw him lean into the thinnest light
that barely held him in relief
against the gray of river, sky, the seagulls
diving, bobbing, flying off.

•

Tough, reborn as "super mom" just past the war,
she'd raised when she was only a child herself
her younger sister, born into the family
nine years late (usurping "youngest"), their mother
sick with "headache" on the couch. The sister—
nuts from birth—would shit while she was in the tub,
her lips twitching even as she bit at them to stop it,
her eyes and all her being, arched-back torso,
flashing through what's settled or assumed,
the socially agreed-upon—and then
denied by fear and hope and covered up.

The mother (mine by now) would call to us
as we swang harder and higher, creaking the frame
until it rocked, her mezzo voice aimed
not so much at us as at her friends and—
confident, seemingly self-assured—aimed also
at herself, where somehow I have always known
she scrambles out of sight, prevaricating left,
then to the right, to side-step any stray
opposing fact, her self-appointed task
to get away with this, to keep the surface
clear of doubt, of danger.

                                        So it's the things
she couldn't hide I can't let go of, spilled black paint,
my footprints crossing the new white rug, a shadow
on my x-rayed lung.

Still, as when I held
my head against her mother's chest, I hear my mother
humming to her mother's humming to herself
those lies I love, the rescue loud and clear.

•

And the bird's sound, squeezed through air
in early morning or at dusk, as light that's seen through oil
or the thickest glass, slowed down so that the path it takes,
its passage, can be traced.

•

How strong, in face of death, the woman seems
as she takes charge where the fumbling staff cannot.

They walk in circles lost, fine troops in white,
then gather at the table where she lies, one breast exposed,

the gash still open, cauterized and smoking.
With the words "It's cancer" out, the eye

refocuses then repositions in an instant every object in the room.
She lets her questions fly like arrows at them.

No answers come, but war is grand. She cuts
them down. They fall like wheat.

Next week they'll hack her right breast off.
She will not weep.

•

Held hostage by this circumstance, like little children
suffering through a first-grade class in reading,
obedient in their listening, hands clasped on the desktops,
faces mocking solemn, they'd look down then up a little,
then back down, ashamed of their distraction, lack
of answers . . . Mother and father, standing there together
near the only window in the room, their features darkened
by the light behind them, nurses whispering down the halls,
the plastic bracelet locked around my wrist, me
lying in my street clothes on the bed—the nurse insisted,
forcing "patient" down my throat, my clothes my only
hold-out. Helpless while in range of me, my parents
seemed to shrink, those usually strong-of-will ones,
hurt by what was brought to them through me.

•

So was it all the fish I ate, the river trashed—
caught and ate them anyway? My legs
dangling over the bulkhead, the sun hot on my back,
its freckles, moles, I fished for eels and catfish,
never thinking of the sun's effect. My mother
cooked my catch for lunch.

Why eating rushed to mind the day they found the "rogue" cells
near my ribs, I can't explain. It was
a different kind of cell, appearing fifteen years
from when they found the first—the cancer
back because I'd had it once? —or from a cure,
the drugs or silent cobalt rays

igniting neck, heart, lungs, and back, my breasts?

•

Black sky grayed in the square of window to my left
as I lay straining at it, and on the other side,
three bars of light through the high-hung door's cracks
spreading barely one foot in. I'd been awake awhile,
I'd never gone to sleep. I moved my legs
against the sheets. For once not startled by the nurses'
middle-of-the-night checks—taking "temp," the pressure
of the blood, the pulse.

Mine had to be racing—going home
after two long weeks of paling against their white, of losing
thirty pounds, of x-rays, CAT scans, surgery awake
and while I slept—woke up to find I'd lost a day.
How could I sleep on that last night, anticipating
what I'd do once I was out?

But getting in the car took all my strength,
leaving me limp and sweating in the sun-warmed seat,
wrecked again on the body's shallow reef.

•

Hairless he came one afternoon, sent
by the minister to "reach" me, my illness
having infiltrated farther
than the flesh.

He walked me to the riverbank where,
allied to the damp gray pressing wind,
I fought him every calculated step
and won.

He died, a year ahead of me in school.
Our eyes met once, but little came of it.
He died, and I came nowhere near
for twenty years

to seeing what he saw—how, never
giving up (you want to live),
it's only fools who don't, at last,
give in.

His body's pretty much gone by now, I guess,
the flesh fallen off the bones,
sifting down like plaster in the walls,
the cheek

I kissed that night we stopped and smoked at the drive-thru.

•

When he turns off the main road
into the tunnel of oaks, my father
doesn't raise his voice above
a whisper, but slows the engine,
rolling all the windows down, thinking
maybe he will join the world outside,
then snaps back into his knowing better,
safer than a lockbox in a bank.

The car coasts through palmetto,
wind-bent oak trunks, arms, and thighs
that tighten around the narrow road
built along the marshes for the view.
I wonder what he's thinking now.
I want to say, What's wrong? But we
keep driving through the oaks

and when we get to the house
he's built up in the trees,
on top of that a ten-foot tower
you can see the ocean from, we climb
all the way up, and sit, and look,
waiting for where we're going.

•

My nose my prow, I cut a clean way
through the crowd,

no reason I can think of for the thrill
of walking down the concrete aisle,
its metal railings' bars a measure

for the towering space: a stadium
become a canyon, and the roar
of human voices, birds—one swirling mass that,

parting before me
as I walk, rejoins behind.

•

Walking each day the street my father lived in seven places on
when he was growing up,

I think: had I been born five years before I was, I wouldn't have survived
to haunt the present now

as if it were my past. "I should have died," I'd say, the "cure" for Hodgkin's coming
just a couple of years

before they found it rooted in me, meaning business. I would wish it,
even, then, to die,

a voice that's distant now, already ghost but, like the angels
in Wim Wenders's film,

the never-born, I'm drawn to places, placeness, leaning close as any ghost
to what it smells like, believing

that I smell it, that I see, and loving it all, the musky earth,
the cracked, uneven bulkhead

at the dead-end of the street, a puff of air that quickens at
the river's face or, rushing

through the tops of trees, exhales its life into them as it passes
unconcernedly

across the sky, the day's moon chalked in white against the blue.

•

Envoi

Just off work, where every move is caught
        and tallied, slipped
into the grid, I stretched out soaking in a pool,
        the hot spring welling
from a rock into a maze of other,
        horizontal rocks.
I was all sensation, all body.
        Then the body
numbed and thinned to nothing, the border opening,
        dissolving at the point
where I and what my edges met convened.
        Somehow pulling out of there
the will to move, I'd switch into a hotter
        or a cooler pool,
depending on how close it was to the ice-cold
        mountain stream
the hot spring fed. I lost my body twenty times
        that night, then dressed
and started back and, without my thinking knowing,
        my body found the pace
and swung, bigger than a body, slung itself
        from side to side—

exhilaration's root beyond a cause,
        it's never what
we think ourselves with thinking into, only
        thinking that we
are that, while at the same time somewhere else
        we're sex, we're ripping,
bolting body brute across a room,
        a parking lot, the space
between us and the sun, or from an atom
        to its blurred electrons,
held by falling into into, spun
        and held at once
—but to what's always moving, being moved.

Acknowledgments

Poems from *The Reef,* or versions of them, first appeared in the following publications: *Kalliope:* "Five years post-chemo, a knife stabbed through" (as "The Horseman"); *Nebo:* "It was no time, it was in a dream" (as "An Accident"), "So what is it, then, this being human" (as "Spring"); *Penumbra:* "When he turns off the main road" (as "Retired"); *Pipsissewa:* "A group of Baptists stood knee-deep in the St. Johns River" (as "Off Heckscher Drive, Fort George Island, Florida"); *Shankpainter:* "Walking toward the ginkgo trees," "He opened the bird and out flew 54 post-mortem bees," "The afternoon I learned a close friend's mother," "You give to them your life to keep," "The rails' sound hurt," "The joy of accidents," "A man who lived near Nagasaki," "Scars still red," "Even when you ask it of yourself," "I dreamed our birds," "And the bird's sound," "How strong, in face of death," "Held hostage by this circumstance," "So was it all the fish I ate," "Black sky grayed in the square of window to my left," "Walking each day the street my father lived in seven places on"; *TriQuarterly:* "Introit" (as "Tempo Rubato 1"), "When you look through air" (as "Swim"), "Here I am a third time" (as "Fall Recurrence").

Many thanks to Lee Briccetti, Ellen Bryant Voigt, Jim McMichael, Steve Orlen, Robert Pinsky, Al Shapiro, Tom Sleigh, and Suzanne Wise for their help with the manuscript. I also wish to thank the Fine Arts Work Center in Provincetown, the Corporation of Yaddo, the Virginia Center for the Creative Arts, Warren Wilson College, and Friends of Writers for their generous support.

Pedagogy, Image Practices, and Contested Corporealities

This volume focuses on popular film, television, and online representations of contested corporealities and contributes to visual culture studies, disability studies, critical pedagogy, and medical humanities. Emphasizing unruly embodiments that transgress and transform, the volume conceptualizes visual culture as a space of query and accountability. In their introduction, the editors underline how spaces of cultural production provide necessary contexts for analyzing the social impact of contested corporealities. Contributors, in turn, offer new perspectives on technologies, disability, and cultural production. Eunjung Kim argues that life-size dolls in contemporary art films show how acts of caring for radically passive bodies can emerge as both erotic and beautiful; Nicole Markotić critiques the prioritizing of death as the most desirable, logical outcome in biopics of disability; and Katherine W. Sweaney's article on the online anatomization of an amnesiac's brain reminds us of the high stakes for medicine and science in the public display of knowledge-making. Working at the intersection of fat studies and critical race studies, Scott Stoneman discusses the body politics of the film *Precious*. Katerie Gladdys and Deshae E. Lott reflect on their lyrical installation about life with mechanical ventilation, and Ann Fudge Schormans and Adrienne Chambon examine how image-making by persons with intellectual disabilities can intervene in ableist-defined social space. With attention to queer theory and transnationalism, Michael Gill considers the British web-based RTV program, *The Specials*, where young men labeled as intellectually disabled fashion their erotic self-understandings as they discuss and appreciate an ensemble of Thai *kathoey* performers. Concentrating on the global politics of organ transplantation, Donna McCormack critically examines feature films that mediate questions of community, ethics, and mobility. The volume is further enriched by an interview in which Danielle Peers, Melisa Brittain, and Robert McRuer discuss the significance of crip possibilities in art and academia.

This book was originally published as a special issue of *The Review of Education, Pedagogy, and Cultural Studies*.

Sarah Brophy is an Associate Professor of English and Cultural Studies at McMaster University, Canada. She is the author of *Witnessing AIDS: Writing, Testimony, and the Work of Mourning* (2004) and of essays in *End of Empire and the English Novel since 1945*, *Contemporary Women's Writing*, and *Literature and Medicine*. With Janice Hladki, she has co-edited the volume *Embodied Politics in*

Visual Autobiography (2014). Her collaborative work includes exhibitions on political video art and self-portraiture (2010, 2014–15) as well as a co-edited special issue of *Interventions* (2013).

Janice Hladki is an Associate Professor of Theatre and Film Studies, School of the Arts, at McMaster University, Canada. With Sarah Brophy, she has co-edited the volume *Embodied Politics in Visual Autobiography* (2014). Recent publications include the exhibition book, *Fierce: Women's Hot-Blooded Film/Video* (2010) and essays in *Feminist Media Studies*, the *Journal of Literary and Cultural Disability Studies* (with S. Brophy), and the *Journal of Global Studies and Contemporary Art*. Her recent curatorial work includes *Fierce*, and, with S. Brophy, *Scrapes: Unruly Embodiments in Video Art* (2010–2011) and *This is Me. This is Also Me* (2014–15).